Ovals

Teddy Borth

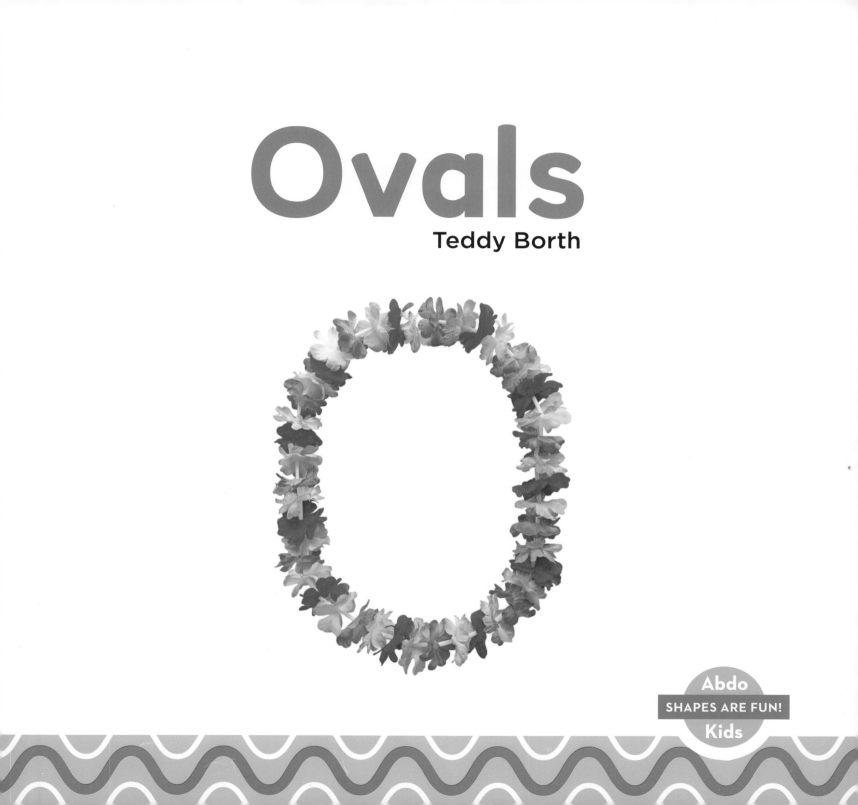

Abdo
SHAPES ARE FUN!
Kids

abdopublishing.com

Published by Abdo Kids, a division of ABDO, PO Box 398166, Minneapolis, Minnesota 55439.
Copyright © 2016 by Abdo Consulting Group, Inc. International copyrights reserved in all countries.
No part of this book may be reproduced in any form without written permission from the publisher.

Printed in the United States of America, North Mankato, Minnesota.

102015

012016

Photo Credits: Corbis, iStock, Shutterstock

Production Contributors: Teddy Borth, Jennie Forsberg, Grace Hansen

Design Contributors: Candice Keimig, Dorothy Toth

Library of Congress Control Number: 2015941977

Cataloging-in-Publication Data

Borth, Teddy.

 Ovals / Teddy Borth.

   p. cm. -- (Shapes are fun!)

ISBN 978-1-68080-144-6 (lib. bdg.)

Includes index.

1. Ovals--Juvenile literature. 2. Geometry--Juvenile literature. 3. Shapes--Juvenile literature.   I. Title.

516/.154--dc23

                    2015941977

Table of Contents

Ovals

An oval is a **stretched** circle.

It has no **corners**.

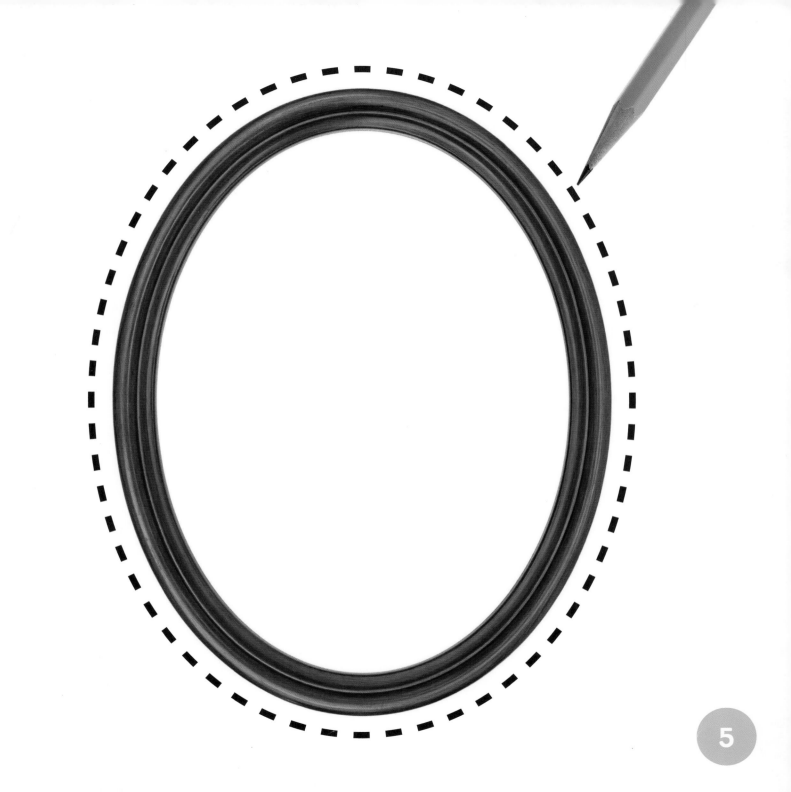

5

This shape is found all over!

Ovals are the shape of eggs.

You play with them.

Kara hits a ball with one.

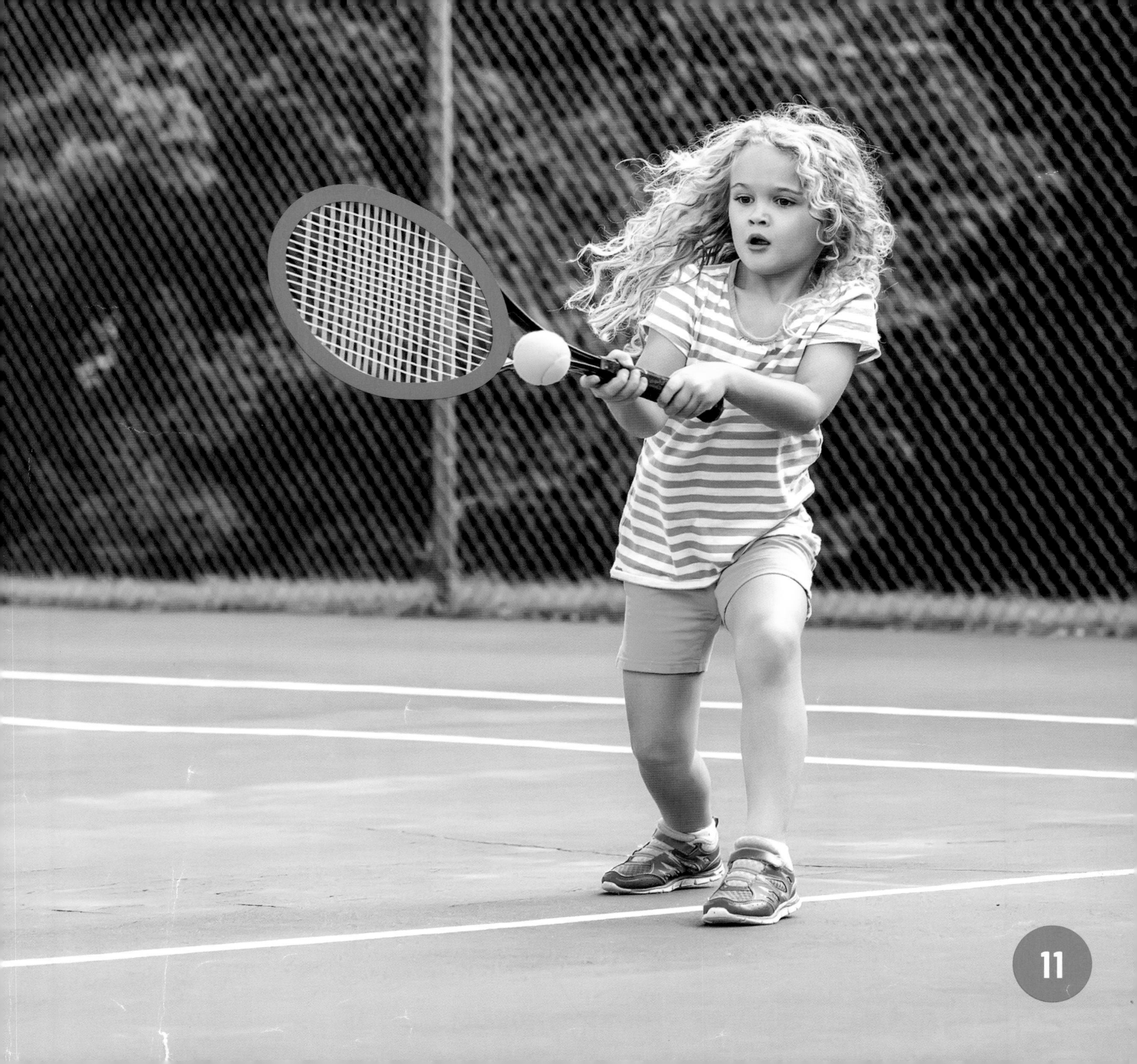

Cars go around them.

The cars can go fast!

13

They are on mirrors.

James can see himself.

15

Ovals are on glasses.

Tom can see well.

They are in the air! Planes use them for windows.

Look around you!

You will find an oval.

Count the Ovals!

Glossary

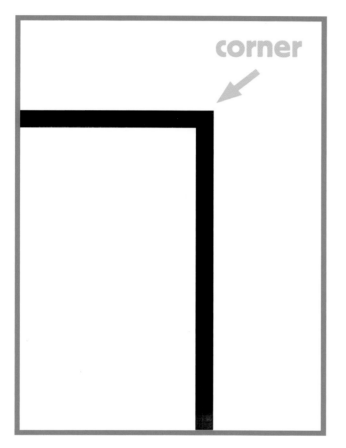

corner

corner
the point where two lines meet.

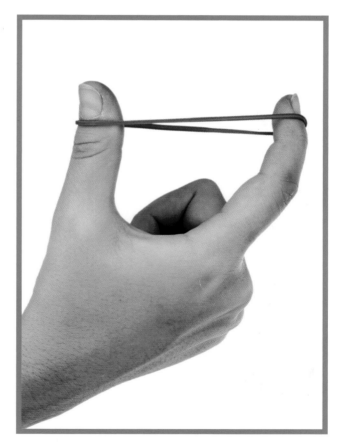

stretched
to become longer or wider
when pulled.

Index

abdokids.com

Use this code to log on to abdokids.com and access crafts, games, videos, and more!

Abdo Kids Code:
SOK1446

24